MW00443960

LEADING
WITHOUT A TITLE

Tim Yao

Copyright © 2017 Timothy Yao

All rights reserved.

ISBN:
ISBN-13: 978-1973927976

ISBN-10: 1973927977

Congrats on being selected as DM! My encouragement to you is that when people are hard or tough on you, it's because they see your true potential and believe in you. Have a great season!

Tim

TABLE OF CONTENTS

ACKNOWLEDGMENTS

This book is a collection of experiences I learned about leadership through the marching music arts activity, but the lessons can apply to much more. A special thanks go out to my parents for their continued support in all my endeavors.

To all the different mentors I had, thank you for the time invested in me, you're all reasons why this book is possible.

-Tim

1. DEFINITION OF A LEADER

Ten o'clock AM. It was a morning that started out like any other ordinary high school day. Except… this day would go down in history as the day that kicked off my pursuit of understanding what leadership truly is. Ten fifteen AM. A United States Army captain announces to my school that I will be the next leader and drum major for the 2011 U.S. Army All-American Marching Band. Of all the things that were said that day one thing stuck out above the rest. My band director said what I see as the ultimate goal of what being a leader is. Thousand Oaks High School band director Marty Martone shared with the entire audience, "When you are young, your actions determine your success. As you get older, the success of your students determines how successful you are."

This book is a collection of everything I learned about leadership, from being a drum major in high school, the U.S. Army All-American Marching Band, Drum Corps International, and beyond. Although these lessons were taught through the marching arts activity, the basic leadership skills can apply to anywhere.

Before we dive in, I want to clarify what a drum major is. If you have been in this position, you'll understand the frustration when someone asks, "You're the drum major? You must be really good at drums!" A drum major is the student appointed leader and conductor of a marching band when they perform their show on a football field. In a parade, the DM is usually the person in front spinning a mace or baton. But at the end of the day, I see them more as a leader than just a conductor.

Definition of Leadership

So... What is leadership?

My definition of a leader is someone who uses their influence to serve others and inspire everyone to better the organization.

There are many definitions, but I sought after a more in-depth description, so I asked a few other key leadership influences in my life to give me what leadership means to them. David Pham, my tour manager during my time with Pacific Crest Drum and Bugle Corps, defines leadership as, "The ability to effectively organize, manage, and motivate others towards a goal or mission." Brian Prato, founder of the U.S. Army All-American Marching Band, sees a leader as someone who "Inspires others to take pride and ownership in a task."

One of the most important concepts I learned in high school leadership from Mr. Martone was that everyone in the group is either an active, or passive leader. Active leaders are those who take initiative and are usually on the front end of making something happen. They are usually your project managers, section leaders, or people with a title. Passive leaders are generally members who take a back seat and let things run their course and merely "survive" in the organization. But leaders can also choose to be passive in how they run things. Being active or passive isn't inherently "positive" or "negative," but understanding how the different types of leadership can influence the group is key to figuring out when it is appropriate to take charge and when to sit back.

Everyone is a leader.

Whether you are given a title or just another member on a team, each person either contributes actively or passively. Remember, you never know how others perceive your actions. In context of a classroom, the teacher is the leader that assigns the homework. It is up to the students to complete their homework. If most of the students are adamant about finishing the assignment, their actions become a factor in creating a homework-completing culture. Let's say the majority decides to skip doing the assignment. This would contribute to influencing others to consider not doing their homework. Basically, each student is responsible and plays a small role for the overall success of the class.

In the classroom example, the primary responsibility for motivating students to complete their homework is the teacher. But in some instances, a student can have just as much influence on others as the teacher depending on what kind of credibility or social standing they are in among their peers. If the teacher is aware that a particular student is causing others to skip out on homework and does not take action, then the teacher is exercising passive leadership and the student is an active leader.

So, with this in mind, when it comes to picking or being picked as a leader, this is something to keep in mind. Mike Freed, one of my music instructors in high school, told me that although my tryout for drum major was before my junior year, the audition technically started the first day of band camp when I was a freshman. Because everyone is a leader, they looked to see who in the band showed potential to lead in the future. No matter what your status is, you are always being watched. Now I don't mean that in a creepy 1984 "Big Brother" way, but you never know when someone may be noticing what you do.

"The Spotlight Effect"

During my second year of Drum Corps, I really appreciated my friend and assistant DM Zach Voth. He was a four-year veteran member and former trumpet section leader. Zach reminded me about the spotlight effect when I let my personal emotion effect my job running rehearsal one afternoon. He said, "Tim, if what happened to you happened to someone else in the corps, people probably wouldn't really care as much. But because you're the head drum major and everyone has their eyes on what you do, you really can't let your personal emotion get in the way during rehearsal."

Having the pressure of always being observed can be stressful. I asked Mr. Martone what are some common mistakes new leaders make. He said that many put too much importance on their leadership instead of all the importance on the task at hand. The best leader is when the members think that they did the task on their own. "You don't win the game by playing it all at once. In baseball, you need to complete the first inning and then move on from there." Often times, young leaders don't break things down in a systematic way that grows success. They focus on the end all, be all.

In drum corps, there was always some issue that needed to be addressed. But as a leader, you're only one person. I had to learn how to systematically break things down to accomplish in a methodical way so as to not become overwhelmed with all the tasks. At the end of the day, when members thought that the rehearsal pacing, logistics, and the entire corps operation went smooth without any hiccups, I knew I had a successful day because all my behind the scenes work was effective. Regardless of recognition, a leader should always strive to serve those they lead."

Qualities of a Good Leader

Servant. I think the most important quality a leader should have is the willingness to be the servant. The most effective leaders I have seen all have the same quality; those that are willing to humble themselves and be a servant. When your heart is set to serve those you lead, your actions will reflect the best interest for the group.

Another quality is credibility. David shared that leaders need to have credibility within a group. This leads to trust and confidence towards the leader so that people know they are capable to manage the difficulties and hardships that all leaders eventually face. "That credibility is gained in several ways, but most often is attained through experience, especially experience in the same activity which the others are experiencing. Others must feel that a leader understands the experience through which they are going through."

Inspiration. I think this is one of the toughest things to master. The responsibility for being an inspiration falls solely on the individual. There are multiple factors that take effect, but at the end of the day, if you can be a positive inspiration, you will achieve success.

When I asked Mr. Martone how he measures success for his band, he broke it down into three questions: Is the staff happy? If so, they will do a better job for everyone. Is leadership happy? Same answer. Are the members happy? Fun comes from being good at something or seeing success in your efforts. If people are happy and have given their best, that is success. With that in mind, an inspirational leader understands what to do to ensure the team is happy and wants to be there.

So what makes an effective leader? Always know why you do what you do. Why DO you want to be a leader or why DON'T you want to be one? In this book, we'll explore my journey and how I learned real-life applications to the different lessons on leadership through the marching music arts.

2. BASIC COMMUNICATION

Let's start at the beginning. During my first two years of high school marching band, I was the kid who just did what I had to do, and floated around, waiting to be told what to do next. If you were to ask me back then if I wanted to be the drum major, my answer would have been "heck no!" So then why and how did I end up where I am today?

Some freshmen come into high school already knowing that they want to be the drum major, while most don't know what to expect and go with what life throws at them. For me, I was the latter and had no idea what to expect from marching band, let alone what a field show really was. This was the time I sat back to see how I fit into the band and tried to figure out what my role was in the group. The reason why I didn't want to become the drum major was because back then, I was shy and did not like standing in front of large groups of people. I was comfortable where I was marching on the field. However, during the middle of my sophomore year, other band members started telling me

I should try out to be drum major the following year because they thought I would make a good DM.

Of course my answer was no, but their suggestion made me take more notice of what the drum major actually does and how he or she influences the band.

When audition time came around, I signed up for the conducting class because by then, I realized that I could benefit the band more on the podium and be a better contribution there instead of marching on the field. I was still shy, didn't like public speaking, and was nervous in front of large crowds. But as a student going into my third year of marching band, I did feel comfortable with being around everyone in band. After the audition, my band director ended up picking two new drum majors, my friend Helen, who was going to be a senior, and myself, who was going to be a junior.

Tradition at my high school was that the drum major who was a senior would be front field, and the junior would be backfield. Ideally, it was set this way so that the junior could gain experience in the back, and then know what to do up front when they became a senior. However, for that particular year, my band director had Helen and I switch off being the front field and backfield conductor every other rehearsal and show since we were both new. Even though we never openly questioned why he chose to have us switch back and forth, we've always wondered what the real reason was.

My band director actually never told us that he wasn't going to pick a front or back drum major all season. So switching off meant not knowing when a main DM was going to be picked, which kept us on edge and really pushed us to be the best we could because we never knew when that decision was going to be made. In hindsight, this tactic was effective and taught us to never settle for complacency. It drove us to really be the best because even though we were friends, the competition aspect gave us no room to be lazy.

Now that I became one of the drum majors, the first thing I learned was how to be a good follower. A good leader should know how to be a good follower because it translates into how effective of a leader you will be. When you're new to a leadership position, understanding how to take guidance from your superiors is important for success.

As upperclassmen, it was easy to develop the mentality of an over-confident leader. After being in the group for a few years, there were times I thought I knew what to do, but actually didn't. I did have an idea of what kind of leader I wanted to be based on the strengths and weaknesses of those who preceded me. One thing I learned from having been in the position for a short while was that sometimes your boss might not always tell you the whole picture. But by being a good follower, I was able to transform into the leader my band director wanted me to be, one that was fit for our high school.

Communication

The biggest lesson I learned my junior year was how to effectively communicate. If public speaking is not your strong trait, I won't go into too much detail, but just give a "basic" version on how to communicate. Three important points to focus on are the message, acknowledgement, and the delivery.

To some this may sound simple, but this was something I had to work on because of who I was back then. During my first few years in band, I was pretty quiet, kept to myself when it came to the grand scheme of things. I couldn't speak in front of large crowds and avoided getting called on in school. I would merely "get by" when it came to doing speeches for class, but otherwise, avoided public speaking like the plague.

If I was called on, I struggled with putting words in my head into concise, easy to understand sentences. As a result, I would talk really fast, stutter, and make the whole experience awkward for everyone.

So this is HOW I fixed my situation and got better. First, know what you are saying. Identify what the message is, and whom you are saying it to. Keep it concise! When it came to the *message*, know what you want to say before you do. If it's on the spot, I find it appropriate and recommend taking a second to think about what you're about to say before you do.

What helped me formulate concise statements was actually learning how to *acknowledge* the message. It wasn't until I became a marching band instructor that I really saw how essential acknowledgement from the band was when it came to teaching. It not only affirms that they heard you, but that they understand. So whenever I was given a message or task, I would restate it. For example, it would not be uncommon for my band director to say, "The battery and front ensemble will be on field 1, color guard will be on field 2, woodwinds and brass will be warming up in sections in the quad, full ensemble block at 4:30; work with Bill (percussion instructor) until then." Obviously there wouldn't be time to repeat all that information, and it would be very annoying if every time I was told something, I said everything back like a tape recorder. Instead, with practice, I would respond with something like this, "Ok, I'll be on the field with the percussion, guard field 2, horns in the quad. Got it, I'll see you at ensemble at 4:30."

By being immersed in this position, the nature of the drum major role taught me to condense the information in my head, and retain it. However, if I was on the podium in the middle of rehearsal, and the box said, "set page 4, we're going from here to page 6," the nature of this conversation is one way, so instead of repeating it, I would either whisper or say in my head something like "page 4-6" Give a thumbs up to my band director, and turn and tell the band where to go next.

Becoming better at retaining the *message* and learning to utilize *acknowledgment* as a tool did not come overnight. I took every opportunity to actively engage myself in each situation to practice getting better at communicating.

The final and most difficult thing I had to work on, was delivery. Despite all that I had learned, I wasn't blind to my own shortcomings. The "Johari Window" model is a good representation of how I chose to approach this. For those who aren't familiar with the Johari Window, it is a model that is basically divided into four sections. These are: Things about yourself that you know are known to others, things about yourself that you know are not known to others, things others know about you that you don't know about yourself, and things that you and others don't know about you.

To improve my delivery, I asked my friend Stephen, who was the tuba section leader at the time, for feedback. I knew I was weak, but I couldn't figure out what to do to get better. So by asking him "how was that?" after giving closing remarks to the band, I was able to identify key parts of my delivery to focus on fixing for next time. It is easy to forget that as leaders, we are not alone.

Remembering to value the importance of what others have to say can help you become a better leader. I approached other section leaders and upperclassmen throughout the season to check up on my improvement. A key thing to remember when setting a good goal is to make it measurable. Halfway through the season, Stephen came up to me on his own after a rehearsal and told me that my closing remarks that day was smoother and that he could tell I was getting better. That benchmark was important because it showed me that I was on the right track.

[A good goal is measurable.]

Another practical mindset I developed as I became a better public speaker, was figuring out who my audience was. The fear of being "judged" was a roadblock for me when it came to being in front of a group. I recalled back to when I was listening to previous drum majors talk at the end of rehearsal. All I wanted to do after a long day of school and rehearsal was just get the information I needed and go home. By realizing that no one was there to judge helped me get over my nervousness and awkwardness. They were my friends, peers, and we were all on the same team. So what did I have to worry about?

In short, with all that in mind, I learned to keep closing remarks simple and offered encouragement. A common mistake I've seen some new leaders make, is that when given the chance to say something, they don't use that time wisely. It is not your personal soapbox time. Remember, you're there to serve them, so whatever you do or say should be in their best interest. This is also why I think it's good to end with an encouragement or some sort of call to action. Not only can it motivate, but inspire people to come back to be even better.

Again, for some, public speaking comes easy. As for myself, by working on making sure I understood the message, acknowledged the purpose and audience of the message, gave a clear delivery, I soon became more confident in public speaking and ultimately, a more effective communicator.

	Known to Self	**Not known to Self**
Known to Others	*Things you know about yourself that others also know*	*Things others know about you that you don't know about yourself*
Not known to Others	*Things you know about yourself that others don't know*	*Things both you and others don't know about yourself*

3. TYPES OF MOTIVATION

Senior Year. I had finally made it to the top of the school! This was also my second year as drum major, and I thought it was going to be easier since it was round two. While I did feel more comfortable, it was also different because I was the only drum major that year.

The most important thing I learned as a senior was how to motivate people. What keeps people going? How do you keep yourself going even when you don't want to as the leader?

In October 2010, I had a presentation that recognized me as the 2011 U.S. Army All-American Marching Band Drum Major. One of the things I mentioned in my speech was how seeing all the band members work so hard motivated me to be the best I could be.

There is a flaw with that statement.

David, my tour manager during drum corps, mentioned the differences between external and internal motivation.

He is a believer in internal motivation because it's motivation that one can control. One of his catch phrases on the road was, "If it's not in your control, why worry about it?" When members realized they can't control the weather, housing site conditions, truck breakdowns, they were able to not stress over things out of their control and focus on what they could.

External motivation can be effective, but when it's not in one's control, it is difficult to sustain over the course of a long period of time. **Internal** motivation ideally starts from one's belief in the group's mission and goal. Why are they there? Why did they choose to be there? A leader should explore to find the internal motivation to maintain and strengthen the group or themselves.

In the beginning of that season, I had an external source of motivation.

The very nature of competitive high school marching band creates motivation for the students through the competition itself. However, ask any marching band or Drum Corps International member, this activity is definitely one of, if not the most "delayed gratification" youth team activity. On average, a DCI Drum Corps will perform close to thirty shows during the summer. During this time, they will spend roughly 30 hours in rehearsal, for about 15 minutes of actual performance time for a single show. That being said, it's easy to slack off and settle for less, especially since the first two months of the season are just rehearsals, and competition doesn't start till later.

With a complacent attitude, my high school band started showing up late, music was not memorized, and effort was not placed forth during rehearsal. The members acted like they didn't want to be there. At this point, Mr. Martone gave the speech that I dreaded. He asked the band what was going on and why they even bothered showing up. He challenged them by mentioning how the members said they wanted to be pushed and have a better show, yet their actions reflected an opposite motive.

The reason I did not like this speech is because it meant that the group was already at that point where the majority of the group lacked motivation and drive to be successful.

A few weeks had gone by since that talk, but there was no observable change with motivation. This is when I came up with my plan of action to try and motivate the group. Now, I knew most section leaders worked really hard and were also stuck trying to figure out how to get the group energy up. However, there were a few passive leaders who were lazy themselves and set a bad example. As a result, many band members emulated their actions. Because we as a leadership team were not moving forward, I called a section leader meeting before our dinner break for a football game one Friday night.

I started by quoting what I said during my acceptance speech and said, "When I see you guys working so hard, it motivates me to drive on." Then I added, "However, when you guys show me that you're lazy, not willing to get better, and after 3 weeks, show no sign of improvement, it makes me wonder why you all want to be here. You say you want to get first place in competition, but also that placement does not matter. You say you want to do your best, yet you don't put in effort. You're leaving your success up to chance. You might as well flip a coin. And since that's what you guys have shown me these past few weeks, I will flip a coin on the podium tonight to see if I decide to start the show or not."

I had hoped that in some sort of last-ditch effort, change could happen sometime before dinner and the show. Here's the thing. Of course I was going to start the show, but I also meant everything I said. During the course of that following week, I did see change, and a more aggressive effort made by the section leaders to improve their individual sections and their section's attitudes.

So, let's take a look at what I did, an after action review. Was my "threat" effective? Yes and no. In the sense that action was finally taken, and positive change started to happen, yes it was. I also had a few section leaders tell me that what I said was a good push for those who needed it, because they knew it was a bluff, and understood my intention of saying those things. HOWEVER, to the few that didn't catch the bluff, and thought I was really going to leave the fate of that night's show in the hands of chance, it was perceived that I was capable of allowing something reckless to happen on my watch, revealing a sense of carelessness.

Like my high school self, many fail to realize that although you may have good intentions with your actions, you also have to take into account how others may perceive it. Noble intents executed with a lack of wisdom and tact can produce a negative result.

[Noble intents executed with a lack of wisdom and tact can produce a negative result]

So what exactly happened that night between my talk with the section leaders and the show? I don't know what they said to their sections, and that's between them, but I do remember talking with Mr. Martone. After the performance, the sections were wrapping up with each other, and Martone and I went aside to talk. It was one of those conversations where we were talking about the same thing without actually having to address the elephant in the room. The dialogue went something like this:

Martone: "Hey, how are you doing?"
Tim: "I'm good."

Martone: "Good. Just wanted to make sure. Well, I don't want you taking things personally. So… Some people are saying things."
Tim: "Hmm…. Yeah."

Martone: "I just wanted to know…. How are the section leaders?"
Tim: Well, most are doing a good job, but some are contributing to the lazy, complacent attitude. I just wanted to offer a little push since after 3 weeks, there was no change."

Martone: "Ok. That's what I thought you meant, and I'm glad we're on the same page because you're absolutely right, just... be careful. You don't always know how people will perceive your actions."

Consumed.

When Martone said to "not take things personally," he also meant that you can't control everything, and that you have to let things be the way they are when you've done all you could. As David used to say, "You can't control the weather, you can't control bus breakdowns; so don't worry about it!" These are all external factors that can effect motivation. The key is to not get trapped in a corner and be consumed personally.

This was actually harder towards the end of the season for me, only because I genuinely cared about the group and the vision it stood for. Seeing people only put half effort made me upset. I'd say this is when I grew thick skin, because whether it was something insulting that was said, or members flat out not showing any sign of caring for the group, I took my band director's words and held to it the best I could.

All of that is easier said than done. So how do you motivate people, even when you aren't feeling motivated? Is false motivation a good tool? Obviously the whole coin flip stunt wasn't as effective as I thought it would be. I learned to motivate others by learning how to motivate myself, even when I didn't want to continue.

When you return to a group, no matter how long you've been a member, there is always a reason why you chose to belong. Why band? Why did I hold the position I held?

This is why I was a drum major in high school.

The band activity helped me grow as a person as well as a leader. The tools and skills I learned not only helped me in band, but also in all aspects of life. Because I saw how far I came, I wanted to see as many people benefit in their own way from this activity.

This is also when I realized that everyone's path to learning is different, and that as long as there is growth, no matter how fast or effective, as long as people are benefiting and learning, it was worth it.

4. PROVE YOUR WORTHINESS

The U.S. Army All-American Marching Band was one of those "too good to be true" opportunities I had the privilege of experiencing. The USAAAMB consists of the nation's top 125 high school senior band members, and performs the halftime show for the Army All-American Bowl. It is free to audition, and if selected, the members get an all-expenses paid opportunity to travel and perform with the best high school seniors in the country for the troops.

When I auditioned, I didn't think I would make it, but with nothing to lose, passing up a chance like this seemed foolish. Whenever I start something new, I like doing my share of research to prepare myself. I looked online to see if I could watch other audition tapes and found a few on YouTube. I then watched them from the point of view as if I was going to pick the next Army All-American Drum Major. This helped me see how others did and what was or wasn't effective in their submissions. I took into consideration the way they talked, sat, and presented themselves in their videos before I made my audition. With all that in mind, I'd like to think that I made a successful application because well, they selected me to be the 2011 Army All-American DM despite my self-doubt.

During Bowl week, I was amazed at how organized the event was. Even though the Army sponsored it, the group was run by its own staff of DCI instructors. With only 21 hours of rehearsal total to showcase a six and a half minute show, the rehearsals were fast paced, and with all drum corps staff, felt like a drum corps with woodwinds.

Complacency

The biggest lesson I learned through the Army All-American band experience was about complacency. During our initial welcome, I got the chance to meet a few band members, and at the end of the first day, I realized that a third of the band was made up of members that were also drum majors in their high schools, which meant they also knew my job. Even though the competition was over, and I had already made it, I kept myself on a competitive edge with myself. Most of my band understood my position, and the last thing I wanted to do was mess up in front of them. And since some of them also tried out for my position, I really did not want to give them the chance to wonder if the director picked the wrong person to be the leader.

Dr. Nola Jones, the 2011 director of the All-American band could not stress enough the idea of "being worthy." There was one particular rehearsal in the Alamodome where we were all tired after a full day and to motivate us, she gave us a pep talk by asking us, "Are you worthy? You were selected as the best in the nation, and right now, I know ya'll are tired, but I know you have more. Are you worthy? Worthy to be called Army Strong? There are plenty of people who wish they could be here, prove to everyone that YOU are supposed to be the ones here."

Getting accepted into the band simply meant we had the chance to prove ourselves to be the best. Just because we were there didn't mean we earned the right to be called All-American yet.

In order for the band to "earn our title" as All-Americans, complacency could not be in our vocabulary. Brian Prato, founder and creator of the group, defines complacency as a success killer. But what exactly is complacency? It is when more effort could have been put into something but was not. Generally speaking, people are inherently lazy. Finding the will to push and go the extra mile takes motivation. I have found that people who settle for only ok or have a "good enough" attitude overall, are usually not very motivated people.

To be a successful leader, you have to be willing to go the extra distance and fight the urge to allow yourself to be comfortable. Being in charge also means you're ready to get down and get your hands dirty too. One of the best motivation tools I've seen to be effective is when the leader is working alongside and doing the same thing as his or her subordinates. But keep in mind that this is only effective if the leader is doing it for the right reason. Understanding when to jump in and work side-by-side and when to delegate tasks will help you as the leader, make the most effective use of this technique.

Brian also mentioned that he "believes in making sure [leaders] surround themselves with people who share the same values and are "there" for the right reasons." What will make your job as a leader easier is if those on your team also share the same vision as the group, and have a solid source of "internal motivation" to help fuel their efforts. Whether we are talking in context of the staff, or the members, having the same goal, despite different ideas of how to achieve it, will help move the group forward.

Every decision Brian makes for the All-American Band starts with one question, "Is this good for the band members?" If the answer is no, he reevaluates and finds a better way. As a result, I've seen this program grow exponentially each year when I return to support Bowl Week.

Adaptability

Ask anyone in the marching arts, 21 hours is not a lot of time for a group to meet for the first time, learn the choreography, add music, and execute a top level performance to be broadcasted live for a national audience. But with the nation's best seniors and with Drum Corps International's top instructional staff, it was doable.

Naturally, there were some parts of the show that I was more familiar with than others. During one of the music rehearsal blocks, the new section of music was unfamiliar to most, including myself. Army Colonel (Retired) Thomas H. Palmatier, former commander and conductor of the US Army Field Band, came up to me and said, "They're all watching you, and they're waiting for you. You need to be confident even when you're not."

Like every field show, there were last minute changes in the show, so during that block, when I wasn't sure about the changes, the Colonel reminded me to keep my composure, and fight the urge to let my uncertainty affect my execution of conducting that rehearsal.

In a perfect world, conductors will have enough time to know the score's backwards and forwards with no on-the-spot changes. However, that's not how this activity always works. Being adaptable, and able to execute something confidently and effectively the first time, even if its new, is a skill that I believe every confident leader should develop.

[Being adaptable, and able to execute something confidently and effectively the first time, even if its new, is a skill that I believe every confident leader should have.]

During the closing ceremony, Major General Mark McDonald, former commander of the US Army Cadet Command, addressed the band by saying, "You've just accomplished something amazing this past week. It is a once-in-a-life time experience, and it was fast. Tomorrow, when you're sitting on your flight home, I want you all, to take 10 minutes and reflect on everything you did this past week. Everything that has happened, everything this group has done, because after tonight, it will be the last time all of you will be in the same place at the same time."

So the next day, I reflected on my experience in during Bowl Week. None of my fellow All-Americans had a complacent attitude; they never gave up, which ultimately led them to be selected apart from the rest of the country. As I thought more about what we had just accomplished, the thought of preparation for the event came to mind. When did they start preparing for this group? I'm willing to wager that when they picked up an instrument or flag for the first time, the All-American Marching Band was not on their mind... because it didn't exist yet! But my takeaway is: You never know how what you do now can affect your future. Don't be afraid to see how far you can go.

[You never know how what you do now can affect your future.]

5. BE THE LEADER

During the summer of 2012, I became the head drum major for Pacific Crest Drum and Bugle Corps. It was a crazy journey because if you asked me a year prior what I thought about Drum Corps, I would have responded by saying it's for intense, crazy people and that I would never do it. What actually changed my mind was the All-American Marching Band. Brian Stockard and Vince Gardner were on staff and also percussion instructors with Pacific Crest. They convinced me to try out since I was from Southern California and it was local. But the main reason why I decided to go forward and audition was because after getting a taste of the drum corps environment through the USAAAMB, and realizing what could be achieved when a group of high-level performers got together, I knew I wanted to be a part of that world.

Now that I've made it into a World Class group, I had to first figure out the difference between marching band and drum corps. Although both activities are essentially the same, the difference in standards and professional mentality required to survive on tour reflected the maturity demanded at this higher level.

The biggest lesson I learned from this activity is: if something is out of your control, why worry about it? This statement is probably the most important take away from doing Drum Corps that literally affects every aspect of my life. For those who aren't familiar with the difference between marching band and Drum Corps, the difference is that Drum Corps is a full-time touring activity that is on the road all summer long for about 3 months.

When you're tired, been out in the sun rehearsing for 12 hours each day, it's easy to get cranky and start stressing out over the littlest things. In the beginning of my rookie season, my tour manager David Pham asked all the members, "Can you control the weather? Can you control the quality of the field we rehearse on? If the bus breaks down in the middle of nowhere, is there anything you can do about it? These were all plausible situations that have all happened while I was on the road.

It's not easy to suddenly stop worrying about something when you've already started to. A rookie mistake I've noticed in those put in a position to lead is the tendency to try and control everything. When you're on the road and rehearsing full time, there isn't an ounce of energy that can be wasted over worrying about something you have no power over.

As a rookie member, the idea of having to "prove myself" to veteran members also added pressure. Focusing on the task at hand was within my control, but worrying about what other's opinion of me was not, and I had to constantly remind myself about that fact. If I had made "people pleasing" my goal as a leader, then I would not have done a good job because it's like trying to hit a moving target.

There was one time during my second season of DCI where miscommunication at our rehearsal site wasted valuable rehearsal time and I became too absorbed in the situation. My assistant DM Zach saw that my head wasn't on straight and said to me, "Hey Tim, it already happened, and you can't do anything immediately to help the situation, so take it easy." I think one of the hardest things for some leaders to do, is to literally sit back and do nothing when there really is nothing you can at the time to help improve the situation.

Another concept DCI members are familiar with is the phrase, "Strive for Perfection, and you'll achieve excellence through the process." The idea that "practice makes perfect" is false; practice makes permanent. It is impossible to be perfect, but if you make "perfect" the standard, you'll achieve something excellent as a result. This is also why Drum Corps rehearsal days start from sun up and end when the stars are out. Every moment is spent trying to be perfect. Also, because practice makes permanent, another mentality we develop is "First time every time." Meaning, you get it right the first time you attempt something, so as to not practice a mistake and make the mistake permanent. This is why we rehearsed so much.

To expand on this concept even further, let's explore the difference between a mistake and an error. Mistakes happen, but errors are preventable. Slipping on wet grass during a show is a mistake, stepping off late because of lack of focus is an error.

As a performer, it is easy to become consumed by mess-ups, but the thing to keep in mind is to identify if it was a mistake or error. If you slipped during the show because the grass was wet, which was out of your control, then don't worry about it, it's probably not going to happen again. If you stepped off late because you were distracted, then that was your fault and you need to take the necessary steps to discipline yourself to ensure you keep your focus in the future. Now, as a leader, whether you are encouraging someone else or yourself, understanding the difference between mistakes and errors will help you from becoming consumed with something that wasn't even in your control to begin with.

[understanding the difference between mistakes and errors will help you from becoming consumed with something that wasn't even in your control to begin with.]

During my time as a world-class drum major, I've also witnessed many different styles of leadership from the staff, guest instructors, and at the DCI Drum Major leadership seminar. Effective leadership has many factors, but I've narrowed down 3 aspects that are within the leader's control. Personal approach, attitude, and character, are key cornerstones in successful leadership.

Personal approach:

How do you approach situations? This is something that some of us may not have thought about before because in general, people just do, we don't always think about how we do. Every situation is different, but understanding how you are as a person can help identify how you will approach similar situations in the future.

Look, we're all human, and no one is perfect. Sometimes when it comes to your personal approach to a situation, there is no "right" or "wrong" way, just a "more effective" versus "less effective" method.

Are you encouraging or condescending? Calm or aggravated? Pensive or negligent? Humble or arrogant? The best way to gauge your personal approach is to find out which trait is more consistent when you deal with a variety of issues.

Try to remember after each conversation or confrontation to self-evaluate how you thought your approach was. Then at the appropriate time, ask others close to you to see if how they see you is how you see yourself… including the positives and negatives. It's imperative to keep an open mind and accept all sorts of criticism. If you find that the feedback you get is always positive or sugar coated, then find others who will actually be honest with you. As you get to know yourself better, you'll start to see more consistency with your view and other's views of you.

Before we dive in, here's a short story about approach and subordinates.

This started out as a joke between my friend and I about the Oakland Raiders. Like any other NFL team, The Raiders is just another football team. My friend was trying to tell me how great they are, and I jokingly brought up an instance where some of their fans fought other fans at games. He defended by saying, "yeah, those are the fans, not the team!" I responded, "What kind of team would attract fans that would do such a thing?" We had a good laugh, but there is some truth to that statement. In context of leadership, what kind of leader would attract certain types of followers?

Positively against negativity

[Leaders aren't there to call out the obvious, but focus on inspiring.]

During my rookie year, Pacific Crest brought in Ralph Pace, a DCI Hall of Fame member known for his work with show design and visual performance. Ralph joined us when we had All-Days, which is when our corps started rehearsing every day before we actually went on the road for tour. After the first rehearsal day with him, I remember

Ralph calling in all of the staff and the leadership. He shared with us his assessment of the corps teaching and learning culture, then shared his philosophy on instructing. Ralph believed in always being positive and making sure the member being corrected understood what he or she did not get right.

The main point Ralph brought up was how he saw the visual staff correct mistakes and their personal approach towards addressing the members. For example, when the corps was learning drill, (where to go on the field) they are supposed to move to their spots with the correct marching technique. However, most new members were not familiar with the bent-leg technique Pacific Crest used. Now, whether it was a veteran or rookie, the visual staff would ream the members for using wrong technique or whenever they went to the wrong spot on the field. In what I've seen, getting yelled at in a drill sergeant like manner works in some instances, but there comes a time to evaluate whether it is actually being effective, versus destructive.

Before I go on, let's not forget that this is drum corps, and that there is a higher standard and a stricter culture compared to normal life. But with any situation, a good leader understands how to read the room, or in this case, read the field. With members ranging from 16 to 21, not everyone is used to the same level of intensity. Instead of changing the standard, Ralph discussed altering the staff approach without sacrificing the quality of education.

Instead of just pointing out why something was wrong and then getting upset for the whole group to see, Ralph's philosophy was to treat the members like the adults they are. The idea was to not just point out what was executed incorrectly, but to explain why, and to do so in an encouraging manner, instead of being condescending. In context of the entire group, if the rehearsal became repetitive because of unfamiliarity, complacency is bound to set in.

Another approach Ralph set forth was instead of always yelling, "That was bad, do it again!" Ask the members if they were satisfied with their performance. Raising your voice at the members wasn't what he was against. Members knew the difference between a loud teaching voice and an angry voice. If the staff could see that something was not done well, chances are, the members themselves could sense the same thing too.

As the manager or superior, when someone does a poor job performance, the employee probably already knows that he or she did a sub-par execution. Although useful at times, negativity is not always the most effective approach. Let's say my friend Nathan, who works at a coffee shop, constantly backs up the line because he is slow at making drinks. Instead of calling him out as an incompetent worker compared to the other employees, a good manager would share with him how to organize a better workflow or give him tips on how to be more familiar with the machines. Leaders aren't there to call out the obvious, but focus on inspiring. Share your expertise, guide those you lead, not condemn them.

"A little friendly competition never hurt anyone."

When the staff and members became more encouraging with each other, a stronger familial bond was formed. Drum Corps is a competitive activity, but whoever said that it had to be between different corps? As a stronger core unit, the different sections would now compete with each other to see which section could reset the fastest, march the best, or sound the best.

All of a sudden, the personal approach from each member shifted focus from "we're only as good as our weakest member," to "we're only as GOOD as our weakest member." It's the classic glass half empty or half full analogy. We developed a positive outlook on that statement and no one wanted to be the weakest member because they wanted the group to be the best it could, not because they did not want to be called out for being the worst and merely survive the season.

As a result, being the weakest member meant you had a lot more potential for improvement during the season, so let's do all that we can to speed that process up. The positive personal approach set forth by the leadership resulted in friendly competition between sections.

All in all, I thought that Pacific Crest had a very successful season in 2012, not just competitively, but as an organization. To my knowledge, most rookies, including myself, felt like they were accepted into the PC family, and that they not only contributed something to the corps, but were also a valued member of the family.

Negativity towards positivity

Summer 2013. This was my second year participating in Pacific Crest, and unlike the previous year, I would show up to camps feeling confident and ready to go. Now that I've completed one tour with them, the early rehearsal camps felt like a continuation from the previous year instead of a brand new season. This was widely due to the number of returning members and corps culture set forth the summer prior. As for myself, one common mistake I have observed many young leaders make is overconfidence. Before we started the season, I had to remind myself that although I knew the drum corps operation, I shouldn't let pride, or a constant "I got it..." attitude take over. After all, complacency is a success killer.

I mentioned how in 2012, the positive personal approach created a desirable atmosphere for the group. However, in 2013, a negative approach almost killed the season.

Between the two years I was with Pacific Crest, there were a few things that changed between '12 and '13. For the most part, things stayed the same except for the visual staff, show design, and new logo. In '13, the corps celebrated its 21st birthday, and it wanted to unofficially prove itself as a "big boy" group worthy of one day competing during finals. From the music, drill, and marching technique, we decided to mimic other competitively successful groups.

Whether or not the staff would admit it or not, this was the culture and theme in the beginning of the season. In the past, many performers would participate in PC but treat it as merely a stepping stone group to reach higher scoring groups. However that year, we had full membership, along with alternates marching on the field.

Everything was set for success from the start of the 2013 season except for one thing… the personal approach from the staff. One of the co-brass caption heads who joined us in 2012, let's call him Mr. Brass, preached the concept of "don't get mad, just focus on getting better" his first year, but that all went out the window his second year. What I think was the catalyst for the sudden change in personal approach was the new visual/ marching caption head. Let's call the visual caption head Mr. Feet.

When Mr. Feet joined during spring training, he would throw temper tantrums whenever the corps did not respond or perform the way he wanted them to. One of his problems was that he was not a good communicator.

Because he could not get information across to the group or other staff successfully, he would get mad. As the spring training months progressed, there would be weekend camps where we would work on a different part of the show visually than we did musically during their respective rehearsal blocks, so that when we came together as an ensemble, we could not progress together as a team.

This lack of cohesiveness led to much frustration because of the lack of improvement. As a result, Mr. Feet decided to tell everyone that they needed to get mad. He said, "When you're mad, you'll actually do something to fix yourself. If you see someone not marching or playing correctly, fix them. Do not allow yourself to look bad."

All those points mentioned above are true. But are they the most effective approach? I think that in short-term, immediate cases, showing frustration as a way to communicate a sense of urgency can work. The only downside is that I've only seen it work short term. On the road, you spend roughly 3 months with the same group of people. Constantly having a negative attitude creates a hostile, and less friendly work environment. Also, while in an unpleasant setting, internal motivation suffers because individuals will inevitably question their membership instead of focusing on the task at hand.

"Are you encouraging, condescending?"

The corps shifted from an encouraging teaching style to a condescending one. The effect of getting "mad" was the bully culture picked up by the veteran members towards the rookies. In the previous year, members would point out to each other mistakes during rehearsal on the field if the staff missed it. Now, members would go so far as to yell at each other for messing up.

Now, how did I know it was the visual caption that created this culture? Whenever we had our leadership meetings, only the horn line section leaders brought up concerns from rookie members in their section. The drum line, color guard, and front ensemble had a stronger family bond with their own, and didn't know what I was talking about when I asked if their rookies felt bullied. Even the tour manager had brief meetings with me about what was happening during rehearsals with him. Since the visual caption works the majority of the time with the horns, it was obvious that he was the main contributing factor towards the bullying going on. Everything else remained constant from the previous season (same veteran members, same brass staff, same section leaders.) Although "bullying" reflected the opposite intention, his personal approach towards the members led to this unfortunate result.

In July, the membership had enough of the bullying. We had a week of rehearsal days in the middle of tour, and it seemed like in between every rehearsal block, a rookie would come up to me that they "wanted to go home," or "quit." I brought all these comments up to the attention of my tour manager, and we decided to hold a rookie meeting. Since it was all the new members, I thought it would be best if my rookie assistant drum major led the meeting. What we actually found out, was that only a few veterans were making the drum corps experience less desirable for all of the horn line rookies through harsh comments on the field.

Never underestimate the influence a few can have on an entire group.

The next step was to confront these individuals about their actions and behavior on the field. David, our tour manager took it upon himself to have a private conversation with the members accused of bullying.

Here's the interesting part. There were two particular veteran members that stood out to the crowd as being the main bullies in the corps (let's call them Derek and Philip.) David informed them that their actions were perceived as hostile and that the rookies saw them as two of the biggest bullies in the corps. He suggested that they watch how they approach communicating with the rookies, and to keep things positive since they were hated. Two people in the same section, accused of doing the same thing, had two completely different approaches.

Fueled by hatred

After being confronted with his actions, Derek took David's warning as the new members being weak, and a bunch of babies. Although he did not openly call out people during rehearsal, Derek would find and tell them in private how much they sucked because he knew the staff had eyes and ears out for bullies when we were out in the field. There was one specific instance where he approached me after a show, and yelled at me for slowing down during one part of the show. What he failed to understand is that as the conductor, when faced with the option of maintaining tempo and having the ensemble fall apart, versus slowing down to keep from falling apart, it is better for the ensemble to stay together. It was a lesser of two evils choice. Had he been a DCI drum major, maybe his opinion and suggestions would have been constructive instead of destructive?

I respectfully responded without raising my voice, "You're a 3-year veteran and I only have one year under my belt. What do you suggest I do different?" The question stumped him. He was so used to being the antagonist and others backing down or fighting back, that he didn't know how to respond. All he could say was " I don't know! Just be better!" I responded by asking, "in your opinion, how?"

This annoyed him even more. All I was trying to do was to professionally find out how I could better serve my corps, so I was all-ears at that point. Derek proceeded to say this, and it took a lot of self-restraint to keep my composure. "I don't think you are trying your best, you don't care about us. Mark (the drum major before me) never messed up like that. We're all doing our job, why can't you do yours?"

There were a million things I could have said as a comeback, but that would've been exactly what Derek wanted to hear... an excuse. Instead, I responded by saying, "You don't see what I do behind the scenes, and saying that I don't care is not only wrong, but incredibly rude. Second, Mark was a great drum major and good friend of mine, but he also conducted and led a different corps." I then went on to explain how slowing down during the show WAS doing my job… keeping everything from falling apart.

After our talk, he walked away frustrated with himself and probably at me too, but not on bad terms. I've always thought that the best way to end tough conversations as such is to find something positive to say and hug it out.

I said something along the lines of "Look, you're obviously very passionate about this activity and that's why you get so emotional when you know we could be better. Just watch how you handle your approach towards others."

What worried me afterwards, was that my personal approach towards the situation kept it from getting ugly. I could only imagine how a rookie would take that kind of verbal beating day after day.

Eventually, there came a point in the season where Derek's section leader couldn't even control him anymore. His personal approach towards other members became a destructive force within the organization. People eventually saw that his negativity was fueled by personal hatred, not encouragement.

Fueled by Encouragement

When Philip found out that the new members viewed him in a negative light, he immediately asked his section leader what he did to deserve such a harsh label. He didn't do so to defend himself, but to identify how to fix the problem. What confused Philip was the "getting mad" concept set forth by the caption head. He said, " I don't understand what I did wrong. I was just doing what the staff was telling me to do. They said to get mad and fix each other, so I was just doing what I was told. I didn't know they thought I was being mean."

The following morning when everyone was out by the food truck for breakfast, Philip's section leader caught him sweeping the entire gym by himself. He said that Philip felt so bad for being a bully that he decided the least he could do was to clean up the corps sleeping area. Philip did this without telling other members because he didn't do it to be seen, but as a matter of principle, a form of self-punishment. Throughout the rest of the season, he would check in with David every once and awhile and ask what he should do to help restore the damage done. Though it was hard for those hurt by Philip to see, they eventually saw that his negativity was driven by a desire to be better, and not hatred.

This is why your personal approach is so important in leadership. How you choose to handle something directly influences those you work with. It's up to you whether you want to foster a positive or negative environment to thrive in.

Attitude:

"It's important to have a good attitude." What does that mean? And why do so many teachers and coaches stress the importance of a good attitude? The words "personal approach" and "attitude" almost sound interchangeable. For example, the sentence "she has a great personal approach." could have the same meaning as "she has a great attitude." But the difference is that "attitude" is the fuel for your personal approach. It is the "why" behind the way you approach something.

The reason behind the "why" is a major factor in your journey. If a leader is not happy doing their job, their attitude not only affects themselves, but those under his or her leadership. During my senior year in high school, when the lack of maturity in the group started getting out of hand, 17-year old Tim took it too personally and let it affect his attitude. Although I did my best to keep rehearsals professional, when I walked to my car, I'm sure my body language reflected the upset feeling and an attitude of a reluctant sense of belonging. It was difficult at the time as an inexperienced leader to see myself in the third person.

A few months after high school band season ended, some of us seniors went out to lunch one day. We were a few months from graduation, and it was a great opportunity for all of us to catch up to see where our future would take us, as well as reminisce on our four years in marching band. I asked them to compare me to my previous year as drum major and to identify some of my weaknesses as their leader. Even to this day, when peer reviews aren't an official thing, I've found it helpful and mature to ask those around to give opinions on strengths and improvements. Back then, I thought my time as a drum major was over, since I had not planned on doing drum corps yet.

Even in a casual setting, I never forgot what they told me that day. My friend Matt and Ben, along with other section leaders, agreed unanimously that they were glad the season was over, and that they could see I was feeling the same way. Our senior show was more theatrical compared to anything we had done in our four years, and the incoming underclassmen were not necessarily set up for success by the show design. The conversation went something like this:

Me: How do you guys feel about this show being our last show ever?
Matt: It was a unique concept, and Joe (our show designer) had us do some crazy stuff.
Ben: Yeah, but I bet you're glad it's over.
Me: What do you mean?
Ben: Dude, you looked like you wanted to kill yourself whenever you left rehearsal.
Everyone: Yeah!

They went on to explain to me how they were all frustrated with the situation, but watching how I dealt with all the drama was both my strength and weakness. According to them, I kept my composure, and they could see that I was always trying to do my best despite tough circumstances. But they could also sense my frustration off the field and when I left for the day.

I was not aware at the time how the members' behavior (external motivation) affected my attitude and how I choose my personal approach (body language) that resulted in others also feeling what I was feeling. My attitude in some ways made me less approachable by the younger members, and fired up those who were frustrated even more in a negative way.

Because I did not want to be at band half of the time, I became a negative influence to the group. Some older members saw that I was upset because I had high standards for the group, but I could not control how some of the new members perceived my attitude towards the band's overall performance during rehearsal. It would not surprise me if a freshman that year came up to me and thought I was disappointed at them and not the situation.

So the big question is, how do you change your attitude when so often it seems like a reflection of how you feel? If a loved one all of a sudden passes away, it's absurd to tell someone to stop mourning and be happy. Attitude is how you choose to deal with your feelings. Keep in mind that there is a time and place for everything. Being the leader is not an excuse for acting the way you want to simply because you're in charge.

[Being the leader is not an excuse for acting the way you want to simply because you're in charge.]

Let's say attitude is the firewood, and personal approach is the flame. You can't have a good fire without good source of fuel. But a pile of wood doesn't simply turn into a burning flame by itself; it needs to be ignited. The spark in this case is your emotion, and the lighter fluid is your maturity, or lack of. In context of fire, maturity can either be a catalyst or an inhibitor. The lighter fluid or water. When a metaphorical "fire" isn't the appropriate response to a situation, then maturity comes in the form of water soaked in the wood to prevent ignition. As for the spark, you can't really control your initial feeling; it's your first natural response. But how you choose to act and deal with it defines your approach.

Now back to the main question again, how do you control your attitude? Towards the end of marching season, when my students develop a complacent attitude, I always say the same thing. "What is the difference between you and the best high school band in the country? They're tired at their rehearsals. They have book reports to do. They have boyfriend or girlfriend issues. What is the difference?"

The difference is attitude.

So how do you "trick" yourself into enjoying doing something you don't want to do? False motivation? When you dive in with an attitude based on an artificial foundation, you know deep down that it isn't real. To a certain extent, this may get you through the moment, but you can only play that game for so long before you realize the reason why you're doing something isn't genuine. You can put on a fake smile and tell yourself that you're "happy" but how long can you put up with an insincere source?

Like what David said, "Internal motivation should start from one's belief in the group's mission and goal. Why are they there?" Again, honing in on the original reason why you're there, mixed with maturity, leads to an attitude that will set you up for success.

If I could say one thing to myself during the middle of my senior year band season, I would say just that. When I did not want to be there, I should have examined why I was doing marching band and why I was the drum major in the first place. The answer was that I learned and grew so much in that program as a person that I wanted to make sure those that followed me got the same chance to grow like I did. As a member, the best way for me to serve the group with the skills I had to offer was to be the drum major. Had I realized that sooner than later, maybe I could have better eased the frustrating times during the season with a more positive attitude.

As leaders, challenges are inevitable. Your attitude dictates whether you will let the challenge defeat you or not. However, I would not suggest keeping emotions out of doing a job. Instead, how can you utilize and control it to help you do an even better job?

During my second year on tour with Pacific Crest, there were many moments where the staff really tested how thick my skin was. That, along with some personal things, meshed together into a tough season. I'm not going to lie, it was difficult to keep myself motivated and fighting to not give up.

Rudy, our tuba visual staff said, "Always strive to get called out for being good." It was a unique situation that year where the co-caption heads could not agree on how they wanted me to conduct, so trying to serve two masters proved rather difficult. But with the encouragement from Rudy, I was able to pull myself together and finish out the season with my head up, knowing that I did my best given the unfortunate situation.

The key to bouncing back is to be a resilient person. Resilience training goes hand-in-hand with your attitude and maturity to move on from a situation. Again, not letting yourself be consumed by a situation will help you look forward.

I wasn't the only one who had a hard season in 2013. But in order to change the attitude of those who also wanted to leave, I had to change my attitude first. When some of the bullied individuals saw my change in approach to the situation, they started re-evaluating their attitude towards the season.

After our last performance in semi-finals, everyone gathered together in a huddle and sang our corps song together. As we all performed Ave Maria one last time together, all the tears came and the strong family bond fostered over the entire summer became undeniable. Once we finished, and emotions were still high, the feeling of relief and nostalgia kicked in. This is when I found and asked the rookies who approached me early on in the season about being bullied how they felt now that the tour was over. They told me that the second half was much better when they tried to focus on being the best they could and tuned out the negativity from certain members. I nodded and acknowledged what they said by saying I had to do the same thing because as they knew, I was also in the same boat as them.

Looking back, I can only imagine how miserable it would have been if we did not change our attitude and let ourselves get mentally defeated in a tough environment. By discovering the real reason why we did this activity, our approach to the situation allowed us to enjoy the rest of the season, instead of merely surviving.

Sometimes, I look forward to challenges because it forces me to re-evaluate why I'm there in the first place, thus resulting in a more pure form of leadership.

Character adjustment:

Don't change who you are for a title, let the title change to who you are. Who you are will come out in your actions. If you pretend to be a certain way because you know that's what the job or title dictates, or you're trying to emulate someone else, eventually, your true nature will come out. Ideally, someone should be able to look at and see you as the example of what a leader is, instead of you attempting to be one. Always be who you are. Be genuine.

This isn't to be confused as an excuse to be stubborn. Good leaders are teachable and willing to improve themselves.

Here's an illustration. Let's say Pete is a young leader who wants to be the drum major because deep down, he wants to look cool to his peers and wants the title to stand out on his college resume. The "why" is rooted from a prideful intention. During leadership sessions, Pete learns about servant leadership, so he tries his best to act like how a drum major should act; Humble, selfless service, integrity, but doesn't feel this way deep down.

The problem is that Pete is trying to be *like* a drum major, instead of being *the* drum major.

Many leaders merely act like the leader, instead of being the leader. I'm not saying they don't eventually learn, but during their time in the position, their true colors show. Maybe not right away, but eventually, through little things here and there, their true character comes out.

For example, if Pete's original internal motivation is based on a "cool" self-image, he'll only do an exceptional job when he knows others are seeing him. If no one is around to witness, he might do a mediocre job or skip it altogether because he is motivated by others and not himself. What's the point of doing something if no one is there to see and give him hypothetical "good leadership points?" The lack of integrity and laziness in this example is a reflection of Pete's character.

The ultimate goal in this illustration is for people to see Pete's character as the definition of a drum major. Unfortunately, he displayed a selfish one.

In this situation, Madi, is also a new drum major. She also realizes that like Pete, being a drum major would look good on a college resume and the title would give her status within her band. However, Madi recognizes that to be the best possible leader for the band, she shouldn't use the position for personal gain.

The difference between the two is that Madi's motivation is founded on the idea of being the best leader for the band, and that the perks of the position comes second. If no one is around to witness her do something, she'll still do an exceptional job because she's there for the better-ness of the group, not for self. The display of integrity and selfless service is a reflection Madi's character.

How...

So now the question is how do you change who you are? How do you transform a lazy person into a hard worker? By genuinely changing why you do something and instilling good habits should place you on the right track towards a positive outcome.

Practice makes permanent. If I'm a lazy person and I am genuinely tired of being lazy, having a source of accountability is the best way to keep on track. Just like how I checked in periodically with Stephen in high school about my public speaking problem, having an accountability buddy will keep you straight when trying to improve your character.

Leaders also need to be teachable. As modeled in the Johari window, there are many things others know about you that you may not know yourself, to include some character traits. Listen to what your peers have to say. I'm not telling you to pursue "people pleasing" with this statement, but to take into account how you are perceived by others, so you can better use that information to fine tune and fix your flaws. "People pleasing" is when your intentions are rooted in doing whatever will make other people like you as a leader.

During my second year in Pacific Crest, one of my assistants was young and desperately wanted to fit in. When the drumline wanted to get earrings, he was peer pressured into doing so. Now, I have nothing against earrings, but if you're put into a leadership position, and decide to use a fake ID because you're not old enough to get your ears pierced because all of your friends wanted to, I don't think that's the best leadership example set.

To me, leaders have to be good followers. Chances are, there is always someone above you on the pyramid. However, even if you're at the top, you still have to be a good follower of your own word. My assistant chose to let people pleasing take precedent over being a good leader.

When your desire to fit-in drives you to make unwise decisions, you're willingly giving up your authority.

I asked David Pham to share some of his advice for young leaders. According to him, young leaders can struggle with making decisions, especially decisions that can lead to dissatisfaction among some within the group. They don't want to anger people that may be their friends or those the leader are struggling to gain credibility.

David also shared a common mistake he has seen in new leaders. Sometimes, a leader doesn't mature in their demeanor and personality when they start becoming a leader. In this instance, he sees a leader wanting leadership powers, but without the work of attaining credibility. The mistake is he or she believes their friendships and status within the group already gives them leadership credibility. It may, at first. But when it comes to difficult situations and problems, a leader must arise above friendships and think about the entire group's interests, which may or may not be their friend's interests. Leaders must remember they lead the group, not just a select few in the group.

One of the most dangerous traits a leader can have is when they think they have it all figured out and have it all under control. That's when reason, teamwork, and rationality goes out the door. There is always room for improvement, so keep your eyes and ears open. Someone who is teachable will be more willing to be a real team player.

6. GAINING SPENDING CREDITS

How do you gain credibility as a leader? Credibility is like having ammunition to execute tasks. If a Soldier only armed with a rifle runs out of bullets, any attempts to advance is next to impossible until a supply drop comes. A leader without credibility loses the ability to command or delegate tasks effectively. In some instances, people will still respect the title despite the man, but a leader should never have to be in a position where that is the case.

Generally speaking, in the marching band world, drum majors are members that either auditioned or are picked after at least one year in the band. Whether people agree with the choice or not, they at least have one season performing on the field to give them credibility for understanding how to do marching band. But what if a freshman that had never marched before was selected to lead?

This is a highly unlikely situation, but what about a marching program that is just starting up? The first ever pilot season of any high school would have to select a student that had no prior marching band experience to lead.

I see credibility as something that can be divided into two categories: *subjective* and *objective*. Subjective credibility would include technical knowledge; objective credibility would include basic leadership skills.

Let's say I was a former construction worker who became the manager of the company. If a deadline was approaching fast and the company was short-staffed, a quick fix would be for me to put on a helmet and work with everyone to finish the project. But what if I had never been a construction worker and knew nothing about building? My options could include hiring more people, extending hours, or helping out myself. However, without the proper credibility, jumping in and doing things may actually hold back the team because of the lack of technical knowledge, and not to mention safety! Assessing the situation and figuring out what kind of credits you have to spend is the best way to make the right call.

In this example, the manager with a construction background has subjective credibility to jump in and help finish the job. A new manager with objective credibility knows how to figure out whether to hire more people or extend work hours without messing anything up himself.

Most of the time, subjective credibility has more spending power because whether the leader chooses to jump in or delegate, the chance of people second-guessing is less because the fact that he already knows what it is like to be on the receiving end, gives him credibility to make a good call.

Objective credibility isn't hard if you have a good personal approach. But it is challenging in the beginning because you can't rely on technical experience you don't have. My first year of drum corps, I was placed in the head drum major position. Although there were similarities to high school and the Army All-American Marching Band, the difference between a "corps" and "band" was still significant. One of the biggest differences was that you went home after band, instead of packing everything up and moving to the next housing site.

In 2012, I had a section leader meeting during the start of move-ins (That's when we rehearsed full-time and stayed indefinitely till the end of the season.) At that point, most of the section leaders were at least 3-year veteran members, and the shoes I had to fill were that of a 4-year drum major.

Since I did not have subjective credibility among the group, I had to build up and prove my objective credibility as their leader in order to run a smooth operation. I stated during the meeting that since everyone had more experience in drum corps and I was new, I was open for suggestions and that if at any time they saw me doing or not doing something that I was supposed to, to come up and tell me so we can be an effective leadership team.

When I first started, I observed the section leaders run the first week of all-days. From managing the equipment and kitchen trucks, section job responsibilities, housekeeping, to corps traditions, I watched how things were run so I could gain subjective knowledge of the activity, as well as assess how Pacific Crest was operated in order to make better objective leadership decisions in the future that would be uniquely beneficial to the group.

Throughout the season, a few section leaders would give me pointers here and there, but still respected my title and let me do my job. With a strong leadership team, from morale to competitive success, I'd say we had one of the best overall summers up till that point. My genuine willingness to humble myself, be teachable, and start from the bottom despite holding a top position earned objective credits my rookie year.

Leaders must be teachable to gain subjective and objective credibility in a new environment.

In 2013, I had proven my objective leadership skills and developed subjective credibility as a second year member with Pacific Crest to be asked back for another season. With both types of credits, our tour manager David Pham approached me during the spring camps for my opinion on a section leader issue that would deeply impact the whole group. Had this issue come up my rookie year, I probably would not have been a part of the solution.

The question was, what to do when a second year member is better fit to be a section leader than someone who already was the prior season? After a brief discussion, I brought up the idea of having co-section leaders for each section to prevent the former section leader from letting his bitterness potentially spread throughout the corps during the season if stripped of his title. Having two would also hide the fact that one was unfit to lead. As for the other sections, it gave them the opportunity to have a previous leader train and lead with the new section leader.

Without good credibility, I probably would not have been involved with that decision making process my second year. The co-section leader plan ended up working very well and section tasks were accomplished more effectively in 2013. By earning good credibility, it helped me contribute to the overall success of the group through my decision.

Generally speaking, leading in a new environment takes more of a conscious effort in the area of credibility awareness. But even as a veteran in the group, it's good to make sure the decisions you execute do not hurt the credibility you built up. It will keep things running smooth.

7. DEVELOPING INTUITION

Many characteristics of leadership have been discussed in this book, but the hardest trait to master is intuition. Webster's Dictionary defines intuition as: a natural ability or power that makes it possible to know something without any proof or evidence: a feeling that guides a person to act a certain way without fully understanding why. As a drum major, conducting, public speaking, maintaining a schedule, are all skills that can be taught. But intuition is something that isn't taught; it's inherent. So how do you teach something that is un-teachable? How do you learn something that is un-learnable?

I associate intuition with alertness and understanding. This is the best advice I can give someone on developing intuition that works wherever you are. Whether it is your first time leading in a group or if you've moved up into a new position, stay alert and take note of everything around you and really understand the "machine" that is your organization.

Before I became a drum major, I never really took notice of where or what the color guard and percussion did during marching band and I had no idea how to effectively communicate or plan anything related to those captions.

By paying closer attention to what they did, their art, their staff, and how they affected the group, it gave me better intuition for my senior year of high school. Running the band felt more comfortable because my intuition from the previous year helped me anticipate what to expect next, even if I didn't always know what was.

Understanding how each moving piece of the machine fits into the big picture will also help you make better judgment calls. With the end goal in mind, anticipating the next move will come naturally.

While on tour, my intuition from the previous year made certain aspects of being on the road smoother. Ask anyone who has marched DCI, every minute counts when you can find time to get some shut eye. Setting an alarm for a 7-minute nap during lunch was a regular thing for me.

So if we were at a housing site where the entire corps was set up within close proximity to the trucks and buses, and we had a long bus ride, the tour manager and I would sometimes cut clean up by 15 minutes or so in hopes that the rest of the corps can have that extra time back in actual floor time for sleep.

Intuition also comes in the form of experience. However, you should never let that trump decisions or jeopardize team unity. Whether you are right or not, it is not wise to implement intuition with a prideful "I told you so" attitude. With the right credibility and in the right atmosphere, using the art of suggestion is a much more effective way than putting your foot down and insisting on doing it your way.

Another thing to be aware of is that veteran members usually want to help and contribute to the overall success of the group. With various interpretations, no two people will always have the same intuition. As a leader, watch out for those newer members who are eager to help but don't always know how. These people have a great heart and I am always appreciative of their willingness to serve.

It's great if you have a new person or veteran who wants to help. My intuition however, is to ensure they are set up for success until they have proven themselves capable enough to not only complete the task, but also teach others.

Whether that means simple guidance or delegating another person to oversee, it's best to not assume individuals willing to help will actually help with their actions. Check to make sure they don't jump in headfirst and realize mid-dive that the pool is empty.

8. REAL LIFE APPLICATION

Chances are, you won't always be in the "lead" position wherever you're at. Just because you don't have a leadership title doesn't mean you're not a leader. Remember, everyone is a leader.

When I started college, I started as a film major, and didn't declare music as a second major until my sophomore year. However, I still played in our wind ensemble and chamber strings my freshman year. During my first semester, I asked myself what my purpose in each ensemble was, and what my role was within the music department. As I thought about all the things I had learned about leadership up to that point, I realized that true leadership, pure leadership, is a leader without a title.

Outside of school, I had been nationally recognized through the All-American Marching Band, and would also go on to become a World Class Drum Major. I had a title and reputation outside of my school, and since my undergrad program was a small institution, not many people knew or understood the marching arts or my role in the marching arts world. I took this opportunity to think through my plan to lead without a title for the following 4 years of undergrad as a musician in our music department.

I decided that if offered, I would not accept any official leadership positions within any ensemble. This endeavor was going to be a challenge. Leading without a title in my opinion is more difficult than with one. If you're a section leader or student president of an ensemble, it's easy to tell someone "Hey, I need this done, have this music learned by this date, this music needs to be copied, etc…" and have it done in a timely matter.

When appointed authority, you are given the power to delegate. But without a title, it becomes much more difficult because you have to lead and influence your peers without that given authority. If you overstep your boundaries, those around may think you're trying to take over, which can end with a negative effect. If you sit back too much, you can come off as someone just along for the ride. This is why leading without a title is difficult. You can't be too much of an active leader, and you can't be a passive leader the whole time either. Finding the line where you're both an active and passive leader was the challenge.

The approach I took was that I would spend the first 2 years observing the music operation of my school, and then play a slightly more active role my last 2 years. The overall goal was to find a way to improve the program in some way or form before graduating. I took note of what the department did well, and what they could improve on. These beginning years were also when I made sure to set the best example of professionalism and standards for the group by making sure I was always squared away, building up my reputation and credit as a musician. This was also when I learned the right balance of intensity and expectation for this college group.

As someone who was a member of DCI, I can say with absolute confidence that us Drum Corps people are absolutely insane... in a good way! For example, when we get music, the unofficial "timeline" for learning is "it should have be learned yesterday." When we get tired, we just stop being tired and keep going. Having 3, four-hour rehearsals back to back, was normal. It's obviously not like that outside of tour, but the same level of motivation, drive, and sense of urgency derived from that life style carries over.

Every year after coming off tour, I would have to go through an adjustment period. After spending 3 months with people constantly pushing themselves mentally and physically for performance perfection, returning to a collegiate setting took some getting used to again. The biggest problem with me was dealing with certain members in my ensemble that would show up week after week making the same mistake with no signs of improvement. In a nutshell, I was used to a different level of motivation and commitment from my peers on tour than at school.

Eventually when my junior and senior year of college came around, I was more vocal with select professors and fellow students, but in an encouraging way to help better the group. For example, there were times I would say to my orchestra peers, "Hey I'm not here to step on your toes, but I would recommend having this done so you'll be ready whenever they ask for the music that needs to be marked up."

By leaving the choice up to the individual, you'll come off as less imposing and more as a friend trying to help. The goal is to stand on the same side and not seem confrontational.

One thing I advocated with string orchestra that carried over to wind ensemble my college senior year was "orchestra dinner" or "winds dinner." I used to encourage everyone in our orchestra to eat dinner together in the school cafeteria after our Monday night rehearsals because I felt like we all played together, but not everyone knew each other well outside. Making music isn't just about producing an enjoyable product, but a pleasant experience, and it's always more fun to play with friends. By creating a time for team bonding, I hoped to help foster a tighter, close-knit group of musicians that actually wanted to show up to rehearsal and make music together instead of simply attending for class credit.

Because of the lack of drive and passion in the group, I thought this approach was appropriate. Looking back to my time in Drum Corps, the love of the activity was a good enough reason to do it, but the people I did it with made it all the more enjoyable, and ultimately more successful. In my opinion, friends make better music with each other, because they aren't there because they have to, they are there because they want to. When people want to do something, they're more likely to be successful at it because of the passion involved.

I took the fall semester of my senior year off when I attended Army Basic Training, but when I came back in the spring, I was thrilled to see that they started doing "winds dinner" before wind ensemble rehearsals on Tuesday nights. As soon as I found out about this I became a big advocate for it because I knew of the potential positive outcome that may follow.

We had a tasking semester with the music selection, but after the concert, when it came time to evaluate and give feedback of the semester, many of us returning members felt that it was one of the best concerts and semesters yet. At that moment, I wondered why that was? We've had amazing people in past years as well, but what made this one stand out. As I looked around the room, I realized that because of our individual personalities and with the slight help of "winds dinner," we all were somewhat involved with each other's lives. That friendship, made us all enjoy and want to come to winds to do a good job because it not only was fun for us to make music, but also offered another time to spend time with each other.

Being a leader behind the scenes isn't always easy. There were many times I felt like I failed the group whenever the concertmaster or section leader would show up unprepared. Those were moments when the lessons I learned about not taking things too personally and not worrying about things out of my control came to be tested.

During my last semester in Chamber Strings, when it came to which violin part to play, my professor Sarah Wallin-Huff, had me strategically placed behind the concertmaster to keep an eye out and make sure he was on track and doing his job. His previous actions and lack of preparation had embarrassed our program in front hired musicians that played in the college group. The sad thing was that the first time he made a mistake, he let it slide, so all subsequent instances became errors, problems that could have been prevented. Making the same error multiple times and using the same excuse isn't a good quality in a leader.

The definition of insanity is, "Expecting something to change without doing anything different." That is why my job in orchestra that last semester, was keep him accountable.

Now, a question you might have for the professor is, " Why didn't you pick someone else to be in that position? Was it something political? Is he the only player good enough to lead since it's a small school?" The real reason was that my professor and I shared the same vision for education. We could have replaced him, but decided that if we really took the time to guide and instill the responsibility and help develop his intuition as a concertmaster, he would be an even more successful musician after he graduated.

If we had simply switched him with the assistant concertmaster, he may not fully understand the reasons why the switch happened and simply focused on the fact that his pride had just been insulted. When you have your feelings hurt, chances are you'll take a back seat and lose your desire to play in the group, resulting in a passive leader. We did not want to take that chance, so we decided to do the hard thing, and actually help him learn to be a better leader by keeping him in the position.

It was in college where I'd say I put everything I learned about leadership through being a drum major into practice. My personal approach and attitude towards understanding the strengths and weaknesses in my college while simultaneously building up credibility from scratch helped me bring about a positive change when I graduated. The confidence I gained from being a drum major in the art of communication gave me the courage to talk to the music department head my last week as an undergrad about the violin teacher that was a negative impact on the string program.

She would bully and demotivate students with her attitude. Her failure to effectively communicate with her students and teaching style could be summed up in the phrase, "here, just watch me." Never once did she explain how to do something.

It was difficult, but I always found a way to motivate myself to not let lessons bring me down. Although she did not have a good reputation, I myself never formally complained to other music faculty about her. I knew this because she would tell me about complaints other students made, and ask me what I thought of their comments.

This should have been a huge red flag, but I protected my fellow students without insulting my teacher's feelings at the same time.

However, it became evident that she was unfit to teach when she broke down during the lesson after my college senior recital, and accused me of being an ungrateful student that did not care about my instrument. To someone who had been playing violin for 14 years at that point, not only was that statement incredibly false, but incredibly insulting after just finishing my recital.

So after building up 4 years of credibility, I cashed them all in, not for myself, but so future violin students would have a chance to succeed in better circumstances.

The result?

A new professor came in the following semester after I graduated and the students as well as other professors all said great things about him. The violin students at the school also grew exponentially. His vision for the music program and motivation inspired students to be the best that they could be. Students looked forward to practicing for themselves instead of practicing to keep the teacher happy.

My original goal of finding a way to improve the program before I graduated was a success made possible by utilizing all the tools I learned about leadership. You don't need to have a title to lead and bring about change.

9. ARE YOU READY?

So, with all the points made about leadership, these are the three ideas that I think are the most important to remember:

1. Always know why you do what you do.

Always know why you do what you do. Why do you want to be the leader? Is it for yourself or for the group? Don't try to trick yourself with the "right" answer. Take the time to evaluate your true intentions. Generally speaking, I've found that people can tell when someone isn't being genuine.

This statement has become a key element in my life. When I first became the drum major for my high school, I had to ask myself this question because I didn't think I wanted to be in that position prior. But after taking time to reflect on my decision, I concluded that I could be a better benefit to the band in that position, and that the duties required were personally achievable. I have seen and met drum majors who became leaders for the wrong reason.

Whether for power and attention, for a good college resume, or for the benefit of the group, there's not necessarily a "right" or "wrong" motive. But the reason does influence the kind of leader you are going to be.

2. Attitude

Attitude is key. Having the right attitude is like the difference between driving with music on versus in silence. Either way you'll get to your destination at the same time, but the journey can be completely different with the type of music you listen to. A major factor into your attitude is also why you're doing whatever you are doing in the first place. Are you going to approach your task with a positive attitude? Or do you need to pump up false motivation to get through? False motivation isn't always bad, but how effective will that be long term? Internal motivation is always more effective than external.

A mature person also understands how to keep their composure, even if emotionally, they are feeling down in the dumps. Attitude influences your actions, and you never know how what you do can directly or indirectly affect someone else.

3. Be teachable

Keep your eyes and ears open, and be teachable. Remember to never settle for complacency. In Drum Corps, we are constantly reminded to "strive for perfection, and achieve excellence." There is always something new to learn or improve on, no matter how long you've been doing it. When you settle for complacency, autopilot kicks in and all of a sudden, you're not giving your best. By not giving it all, the level of the group doesn't stay stagnant; it gets worse because the bar is always moving forward.

Everything else mentioned in earlier chapters in regards to communication, motivation, character, intuition, mentality, etc. are all important, but I think effective leadership can be covered if you understand the why, attitude, and the ability to improve.

I hope these lessons I learned are helpful and offer a new perspective on leadership. With that in mind, here's why I do what I do. My dedication to music and the marching arts community is to use the activity as a way to teach the tools and skills necessary for success. Whatever my students go on to do, the goal is for them to be leaders and an inspiration wherever they are.

ABOUT THE AUTHOR

I decided to write a book on leadership in 2009, after realizing all the valuable lessons I learned as the drum major for Thousand Oaks High School.

After becoming the 2011 U.S. Army All-American Marching Band Drum Major as a high school senior, I knew in order for my book to be truly successful, I needed more experience and credibility, which became one of the deciding factors for me to audition and participate in Drum Corps International.

I made sure to journal and document each day in DCI, so as to not leave out any important details from tour.

Each fall when I got off tour, I was eager to apply things I learned in the summer to my time in college, but stuck to my personal challenge of leading without a title.

In 2014, I decided to join the U.S. Army during the summer between my junior and senior year of college. Though I did not make much reference in this book, I also took on the same challenge on becoming a leader without a title within my basic training platoon. Like my time in DCI, I documented each day, and maybe someday I'll publish something about all of my military experience.

Currently, I'm working with several marching bands in the Southern California area and really enjoyed my time as a high school band director, while also simultaneously building up my Film and TV career outside of music.

Thanks for all the support!
-Tim

leading.without.a.title@gmail.com

66683094R00062

Made in the USA
San Bernardino, CA
15 January 2018